CCSS Genre **Tall Tale**

Essential Question
What are some reasons people moved west?

The TALE of JOHN HENRY

by **Bill Nagelkerke** | illustrated by **Carlo Molinari**

Chapter 1
ON GRANDMA POLLY'S PORCH

"Gather around, you two young ones, gather around!" After calling out this command, Grandma Polly settled back into her rocker on the porch.

Grandma Polly was elderly, and she rested often. Sam was used to that, just as he was used to helping out around his grandmother's place.

Sam lived just a few houses away, and he was at Grandma Polly's most afternoons and evenings. He liked helping her cook her dinner, and sometimes he even washed up.

Sam's cousin Josiah had only visited a handful of times because he lived a few stations down the line. This weekend was one of those times. It had not been easy for Sam because Josiah questioned just about everything Grandma Polly and Sam said.

"What's all that about?" Josiah asked Sam when he heard Grandma Polly's call.

"Grandma is going to tell us a story," Sam explained. "She tells me a story every night before I go home."

"Who needs stories anyway?" scoffed Josiah. "What I'd like now more than anything is a cool drink."

Sam did not say anything, but he knew Grandma Polly did not like to be kept waiting. Josiah knew that he had to do what his cousin did because that was one of the rules of visiting their grandmother.

Josiah sighed and followed Sam. They both climbed the steps onto Grandma Polly's porch.

Grandma Polly had brought out three tumblers of homemade lemonade. "Help yourselves, boys," she said.

Sam and Josiah each took a tumbler, and Josiah sighed again. It had been such a hot day that even the grass had withered in the summer heat.

"This reminds me of the time your granddaddy drove the steel," said Grandma Polly, wiping away the beads of perspiration that had gathered on her forehead.

Josiah looked sideways at Sam and whispered, "What does she mean?"

Sam grinned because he knew this particular story extremely well. Grandma Polly had told it numerous times, but it was still his favorite tale. He could tell it almost as well as his grandma, and in fact, they often shared the telling.

When Sam looked up at Grandma Polly, she gave him a nod. Sam began the story in the exact same way she always did.

"It was in the days," Sam said and then waited for Grandma Polly to carry on.

"In what days?" Josiah asked, forgetting to whisper.

"Don't interrupt, young man," said Grandma Polly. "It means in the long ago days—in the days of my beloved John Henry."

"Our granddaddy," said Sam, his voice full of pride.

"It was in the days when people were on the move," Grandma Polly said. "The prospector, the railroad worker, the traveling salesman, husbands, wives, and children—they were all on the move. And my John Henry was on the move, too."

Grandma Polly continued, "He had been enslaved, but now he was free, and he was looking for work. In those days, the travel was long and arduous, so that's why people began to build the railroads. Long lines of iron and steel joined up the territories of the whole of the United States, settlement by settlement."

"I came here by train," said Josiah, "but it wasn't very far …"

"Hush!" said Sam. "Listen to the story."

Josiah glared at Sam for telling him to be quiet, but he did stop talking.

Chapter 2

THE STEEL-DRIVING MAN

"John Henry was the biggest railroad man who ever lived," said Sam, continuing the story. "The biggest and the best!"

Grandma Polly added, "He was tall like an oak tree and broad like a barn, stronger than a dozen men, and handsomer than any other man. He was—"

"A steel driver," said Sam. "That means," he said quickly, before Josiah had the chance to ask, "someone who hammered steel rods into the mountainside so the workers could blast away the stone and lay the railroad tracks."

"Did they blast away the mountain with dynamite?" asked Josiah, his eyes lighting up at the thought.

"Yes," answered Grandma Polly, "they put the dynamite in the holes my John Henry made."

"And then BOOM!" said Sam. "Our granddaddy was the most powerful steel driver they had. It was dangerous work, and it was hard work, but Granddaddy was generous, too—if the other men got tired, he'd step in and finish what they'd started."

"He hammered long steel rods into solid rock—can you imagine that?" asked Grandma Polly. "My John Henry could move mountains, and that's the truth."

"I don't believe—" began Josiah, unable to help himself.

Sam tried to quiet him, but Grandma Polly had heard him. She looked at Josiah with a twinkle in her eye.

"If you don't believe me, young man," she said, "then I will prove it to you."

When Josiah asked her how she would prove that John Henry could move mountains, Grandma Polly said, "Sam, why don't you show your cousin."

Sam stood up and went inside.

Josiah watched Sam disappear indoors and then asked where his cousin had gone.

Grandma Polly replied with a look that said, "Wait and see, young man, wait and see."

Soon enough Sam returned, carrying a heavy rod of steel that was taller than Sam.

"Wow!" said Josiah, clearly impressed. "Can I have a turn at lifting that?"

Sam passed Josiah the rod and said, "That's what Granddaddy hammered into the mountainside."

"It's a mighty thing," Josiah replied, feeling the rod.

Sam looked at Grandma Polly, and she returned his gaze with a nod. Sam went back inside, and when he returned, he was dragging something very heavy.

"What's that?" asked Josiah.

"That's the hammer John Henry used for hammering in the rods," said Grandma Polly.

"Can I have a turn at lifting that?" asked Josiah, jumping up.

"You can try," said Sam, "but I can't lift it, so I bet you won't be able to, either."

Josiah heaved with all his might, but he couldn't raise the enormous hammer a single inch.

"Now do you want to hear what happened next?" asked Sam.

Josiah no longer scoffed but instead nodded and said, "I guess."

"No need to guess, young man—I'll tell you," said Grandma Polly. "It happened after John Henry and I met and got married... Not long after that, it all went wrong."

Grandma Polly paused and then became silent. Josiah noticed a tear run from the corner of her eye.

"What happened next?" Josiah mouthed, turning to Sam.

Chapter 3

THE TRAVELING SALESMAN

Sam realized that his grandma was upset, so he was the first to speak. "What happened next was something terrible."

"I can't imagine," Josiah said.

"Wait and listen," Grandma Polly suggested, her voice quiet and her eyes full of tears.

Grandma Polly looked down at Sam and signaled for him to continue telling the tale.

"Well, what happened next was that one day a traveling salesman turned up at the mountainside," said Sam.

"The mountainside where Granddaddy worked?"

"The very same," said Sam. "They were building a tunnel through the mountain, and hundreds of men were driving the steel and moving the stone."

"When the wind was blowing in my direction, I could hear the noise they made from my porch," said Grandma Polly.

Sam continued, "All this salesman was interested in was selling stuff and making money—and making a point of winning."

"My daddy's a salesman," said Josiah, a note of hurt in his voice.

"Your daddy is nothing like this man was," said Grandma Polly. "They're as different as fire and ice, I'm telling you."

"This salesman was a miserable fellow," said Sam. "Maybe the heat and dust made him that way."

"So, what was this miserable sales fellow selling?" asked Josiah.

"He wanted to sell the railroad company something called a steam drill."

Josiah looked puzzled. "A what?"

"A steam drill did the same work as a man with a hammer and rod," Sam explained. "Only, the salesman said, his machine could hammer the rod faster than a man could, and it could do the work of many men. He said, 'Who needs men to do the work when a machine can do it better, faster, and cheaper?'"

"Some machines can—" began Josiah.

Sam didn't give his cousin time to finish that sentence—it was as if the story of John Henry had taken him over.

"And Granddaddy," said Sam, "when he heard the salesman's talk, he said that no machine was better or faster or cheaper than him. They didn't pay enough money as it was. The other men laughed at this. The salesman just laughed, too, and then he challenged Granddaddy to a contest."

Grandma Polly began to move back and forth on the rocking chair, and as she did, the floorboards squeaked, sounding high and ghostly, like thin whistles coming from far away. The wind rose and blew softly into their faces.

"I can still hear his hammer pounding and the steam drill hissing," said Grandma Polly.

Josiah looked up at her, his mouth wide open.

"The salesman said that if Granddaddy could beat the steam drill, then the railroad company could have the drill for free," said Sam.

"I told him not to do it," whispered Grandma Polly from her rocking chair.

Sam stood up and put his arm around his grandma.

"But he had to," she said to the boys, "because he didn't want those men to lose their jobs. So he took up his hammer and set to work."

Chapter 4

THE CONTEST

"The day of the contest was fiery hot like today, as if there were a fever in the air," continued Sam.

"Did the grass shrivel up?' asked Josiah.

"It sure did," Sam replied, "and the mountain was colored tawny, like a dusty mountain lion."

"When the contest started," continued Sam, "John Henry and the steam drill set to work. Granddaddy was hammering so fast, plunging the rods into that solid rock. Dust and dirt rose into the air, and people were sweating and choking. 'Stop, John Henry, stop!' they shouted, because they could see Granddaddy swaying on his feet."

"Why didn't he stop?" asked Josiah.

"Because he was our granddaddy—the biggest, strongest, and most determined man alive. He hammered in the rods faster and faster, then he grabbed up another hammer. Now he was wielding a hammer in each hand."

"Did the steam drill beat him?" Josiah asked.

"The steam drill sputtered and steamed and drilled down deep, but it never drilled as fast or as far as John Henry did," said Grandma Polly, taking up the tale again. "My John Henry won that battle."

"I just knew he would win!" said Josiah.

"He won the battle, but he lost the war," Grandma Polly said.

"What does that mean?" Josiah asked.

"It means," said Sam, "that the contest killed Granddaddy. His brave heart burst, he toppled over, and then he died."

They were all quiet then.

Eventually, Josiah broke the silence, "That story is so sad, but it makes me wish I'd met Granddaddy."

A cricket chirruped, a frog croaked, and a train whistled. Soon the train went by with a rush and a roar.

"It's heading for the tunnel Granddaddy helped build," said Sam.

"I'd love to see it," said Josiah.

"Let's go along and look tomorrow—it's not far from here," said Sam.

"I might even come with you," said Grandma Polly. "It's sad to remember, but it's best not to forget."

"There're plenty of stories about John Henry," said Sam.

"Once you hear a story, it belongs to you forever," said Grandma Polly, "and stories never die."

Respond to Reading

Summarize

Use important details from the story to summarize *The Tale of John Henry*. Your graphic organizer may help you.

Cause → Effect
→
→
→
→

Text Evidence

1. Why is *The Tale of John Henry* a tall tale? Use details from the story to explain. **GENRE**

2. Why does John Henry compete against the steam drill? **CAUSE AND EFFECT**

3. Josiah sees a tear run down Grandma Polly's face on page 9. Use context clues to define the homograph *tear* in that sentence. What does *tear* mean when it is used as a verb? **HOMOGRAPHS**

4. Write about what happened after the salesman challenged John Henry to a contest with the steam drill. **WRITE ABOUT READING**

Compare Texts
Read about the building of the transcontinental
railroad in the 1860s.

The
Transcontinental Railroad

When gold was discovered in California in 1848, more and more people wanted to travel west. However, traveling across the United States was difficult. People endured many dangers crossing deserts and mountains by wagon. It could take six months to reach California.

A railroad would be a faster, safer, and more reliable way of traveling west. It would allow people to settle in different parts of the country. Farmers would be able to transport their goods more easily.

The government decided to build a transcontinental railroad that would connect the east coast of the United States with the west coast.

Work on the transcontinental railroad began in 1863. The government hired two companies to build the railroad. The Union Pacific Railroad company would build westward from Omaha, Nebraska, while the Central Pacific Railroad company would build eastward from Sacramento, California. The railroad tracks would meet in Promontory, Utah.

The transcontinental railroad was a major engineering feat. New techniques had to be developed, and new skills had to be learned to build the railroad.

The terrain was difficult, and so was the weather. In winter it snowed, and in summer it was scorching hot. It was easier to lay tracks and run trains on flat land. Small hills were cut to make the track level. Tunnels were blasted through mountains using dynamite.

The Transcontinental Railroad Route

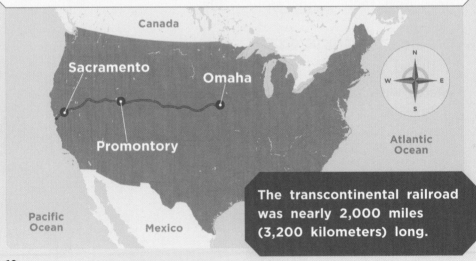

The transcontinental railroad was nearly 2,000 miles (3,200 kilometers) long.

A crowd watches the final spike being driven in on the transcontinental railroad.

The Workers

Thousands of people helped build the transcontinental railroad—laying tracks, hammering in spikes, and building bridges. Many soldiers who had fought in the American Civil War (1861–1865) helped construct the railroad. Other workers came from countries such as Ireland and China. The work was long, hard, and dangerous. Many workers died in rockslides and blasting accidents.

The Final Spike

Despite all the difficulties, the transcontinental railroad was finished in just six years. In 1869, the final spike was hammered in place at Promontory, Utah.

Make Connections

How did the building of the transcontinental railroad help the settlement of the west?

ESSENTIAL QUESTION

Why do you think people told tall tales such as the story of John Henry's contest with the steam drill?

TEXT TO TEXT

Focus on Genre

Tall Tales Tall tales are stories about people who are supposed to have done incredible things. The heroes of these tales often had great physical strength in a time when life was hard. Sometimes a tall tale may be based on the life of a real person, but the person's feats are greatly exaggerated.

Read and Find This tall tale is full of examples of exaggerated feats performed by the main character. John Henry "was tall like an oak tree and broad like a barn, stronger than a dozen men ..." (page 6). Grandma Polly says he "could move mountains, and that's the truth" (page 7).

Your Turn

With a partner, role-play a situation in which the steam-drill salesman is on trial for causing the death of John Henry. One person plays the part of the prosecuting lawyer, asking the salesman questions about the contest. The other person plays the salesman, explaining why he suggested the challenge.

Use your questions and answers to write a summation to the jury by the lawyer arguing why the salesman should be found guilty or not guilty. Read your summation to the class.